Faith *Notes*
Devotional
JOURNAL

BARBOUR

PUBLISHING

Published by Barbour Publishing, Inc., P.O. Box 719, Uhrichsville, Ohio 44683, www.barbourbooks.com

Our mission is to publish and distribute inspirational products offering exceptional value and biblical encouragement to the masses.

Member of the
Evangelical Christian
Publishers Association

Printed in China.

Expect great things from God.
Attempt great things for God.
WILLIAM CAREY

And we know that in all things God works for the good of those who love him, who have been called according to his purpose.
ROMANS 8:28 NIV

Date and Time: ....

Place: ....

Today's Devotional Topic: ....

....

Notes: ....

....

....

....

....

....

....

....

....

....

My Personal Thoughts:

_____

_____

_____

_____

_____

_____

_____

Key Bible Verses:

_____

_____

_____

_____

_____

_____

_____

_____

_____

_____

No one has ever seen God; but if we love one another,
God lives in us and his love is made complete in us.
1 JOHN 4:12 NIV

Date and Time:

Place:

Today's Devotional Topic:

Notes:

My Personal Thoughts: _____

_____

_____

_____

_____

_____

_____

_____

Key Bible Verses: _____

_____

_____

_____

_____

_____

_____

_____

_____

*Trust should be in God who richly gives us all
we need for our enjoyment.*
1 TIMOTHY 6:17 NLT

Date and Time: ....

Place: ....

Today's Devotional Topic: ....

....

Notes: ....

....

....

....

....

....

....

....

....

....

....

My Personal Thoughts:

Key Bible Verses:

*Being confident of this, that he who began a good work in you
will carry it on to completion until the day of Christ Jesus.*
PHILIPPIANS 1:6 NIV

Date and Time:

Place:

Today's Devotional Topic:

Notes:

My Personal Thoughts:

_____

_____

_____

_____

_____

_____

_____

Key Bible Verses:

_____

_____

_____

_____

_____

_____

_____

_____

_____

Having hope will give you courage.
You will be protected and will rest in safety.
JOB 11:18 NLT

Date and Time:

Place:

Today's Devotional Topic:

Notes:

My Personal Thoughts:

Key Bible Verses:

> *"Be strong and courageous, and act;*
> *do not fear nor be dismayed,*
> *for the LORD God, my God, is with you.*
> *He will not fail you nor forsake you."*
> 1 CHRONICLES 28:20 NASB

Date and Time: ....

Place: ....

Today's Devotional Topic: ....

....

Notes: ....

....

....

....

....

....

....

....

....

....

My Personal Thoughts:

Key Bible Verses:

But the eyes of the LORD are on those who fear him,
on those whose hope is in his unfailing love.
PSALM 33:18 NIV

Date and Time:

Place:

Today's Devotional Topic:

Notes:

My Personal Thoughts:

Key Bible Verses:

> *"Blessed are the poor in spirit, for theirs
> is the kingdom of heaven."*
> MATTHEW 5:3 NASB

Date and Time: ....

Place: ....

Today's Devotional Topic: ....
....

Notes: ....
....
....
....
....
....
....
....
....
....
....

My Personal Thoughts:

_____

_____

_____

_____

_____

_____

_____

Key Bible Verses:

_____

_____

_____

_____

_____

_____

_____

_____

_____

Our comfort is abundant through Christ.
2 CORINTHIANS 1:5 NASB

Date and Time: ....

Place: ....

Today's Devotional Topic: ....

....

Notes: ....

....

....

....

....

....

....

....

....

My Personal Thoughts:

Key Bible Verses:

We rejoice in the hope of the glory of God.
ROMANS 5:2 NIV

Date and Time: ....

Place: ....

Today's Devotional Topic: ....

....

Notes: ....

....

....

....

....

....

....

....

....

....

....

My Personal Thoughts:

Key Bible Verses:

"My grace is sufficient for you,
for my power is made perfect in weakness."
2 CORINTHIANS 12:9 NIV

Date and Time: ....

Place: ....

Today's Devotional Topic: ....

....

Notes: ....

....

....

....

....

....

....

....

....

....

My Personal Thoughts:

_____

_____

_____

_____

_____

_____

_____

Key Bible Verses:

_____

_____

_____

_____

_____

_____

_____

_____

_____

O God, we give glory to you all day long
and constantly praise your name.
PSALM 44:8 NLT

Date and Time:

Place:

Today's Devotional Topic:

Notes:

My Personal Thoughts:

Key Bible Verses:

*"Go into all the world
and preach the gospel to all creation."*
MARK 16:15 NASB

Date and Time: ....

Place: ....

Today's Devotional Topic: ....

....

Notes: ....

....

....

....

....

....

....

....

....

....

My Personal Thoughts:

_____

_____

_____

_____

_____

_____

_____

Key Bible Verses:

_____

_____

_____

_____

_____

_____

_____

_____

_____

Lead me by your truth and teach me,
for you are the God who saves me.
All day long I put my hope in you.
PSALM 25:5 NLT

Date and Time:

Place:

Today's Devotional Topic:

Notes:

My Personal Thoughts:

_____

_____

_____

_____

_____

_____

_____

_____

Key Bible Verses:

_____

_____

_____

_____

_____

_____

_____

_____

_____

_____

Three things will last forever—
faith, hope, and love.
1 CORINTHIANS 13:13 NLT

Date and Time: _____

Place: _____

Today's Devotional Topic: _____

_____

Notes: _____

_____

_____

_____

_____

_____

_____

_____

_____

_____

My Personal Thoughts:

_____

_____

_____

_____

_____

_____

_____

Key Bible Verses:

_____

_____

_____

_____

_____

_____

_____

_____

*Always giving thanks to God the Father for everything,
in the name of our Lord Jesus Christ.*
EPHESIANS 5:20 NIV

Date and Time:

Place:

Today's Devotional Topic:

Notes:

My Personal Thoughts:

Key Bible Verses:

The joy of the LORD is your strength.
NEHEMIAH 8:10 KJV

Date and Time:

Place:

Today's Devotional Topic:

Notes:

My Personal Thoughts: _____

_____

_____

_____

_____

_____

_____

_____

_____

Key Bible Verses: _____

_____

_____

_____

_____

_____

_____

_____

_____

_____

Be anxious for nothing, but in everything
by prayer and supplication
with thanksgiving let your requests
be made known to God.
PHILIPPIANS 4:6 NASB

Date and Time:

Place:

Today's Devotional Topic:

Notes:

My Personal Thoughts:

_____

_____

_____

_____

_____

_____

_____

Key Bible Verses:

_____

_____

_____

_____

_____

_____

_____

_____

_____

_____

Commit everything you do to the LORD.
PSALM 37:5 NLT

Date and Time:

Place:

Today's Devotional Topic:

Notes:

My Personal Thoughts:

Key Bible Verses:

Just as you received Christ Jesus as Lord,
continue to live in him, rooted and built up in him,
strengthened in the faith as you were taught,
and overflowing with thankfulness.
COLOSSIANS 2:6–7 NIV

Date and Time:

Place:

Today's Devotional Topic:

Notes:

My Personal Thoughts:

_____

_____

_____

_____

_____

_____

_____

Key Bible Verses:

_____

_____

_____

_____

_____

_____

_____

_____

Delight yourself in the LORD
and he will give you the desires of your heart.
PSALM 37:4 NIV

Date and Time:

Place:

Today's Devotional Topic:

Notes:

My Personal Thoughts:

_____

_____

_____

_____

_____

_____

_____

Key Bible Verses:

_____

_____

_____

_____

_____

_____

_____

_____

_____

"Be still, and know that I am God."
PSALM 46:10 NIV

Date and Time: ....

Place: ....

Today's Devotional Topic: ....

....

Notes: ....

....

....

....

....

....

....

....

....

....

My Personal Thoughts:

_____

_____

_____

_____

_____

_____

_____

Key Bible Verses:

_____

_____

_____

_____

_____

_____

_____

_____

_____

This is the day the LORD has made;
let us rejoice and be glad in it.
PSALM 118:24 NIV

Date and Time:

Place:

Today's Devotional Topic:

Notes:

My Personal Thoughts:

_____

_____

_____

_____

_____

_____

_____

Key Bible Verses:

_____

_____

_____

_____

_____

_____

_____

_____

_____

Praise ye the LORD. Praise God in his sanctuary:
praise him in the firmament of his power.
Praise him for his mighty acts:
praise him according to his excellent greatness. . . .
Let every thing that hath breath praise the LORD.
Praise ye the LORD.
PSALM 150:1–2, 6 KJV

Date and Time: ....

Place: ....

Today's Devotional Topic: ....

....

Notes: ....

....

....

....

....

....

....

....

....

....

My Personal Thoughts:

Key Bible Verses:

It is of the LORD's mercies that we are not consumed,
because his compassions fail not.
They are new every morning: great is thy faithfulness.
LAMENTATIONS 3:22–23 KJV

Date and Time:

Place:

Today's Devotional Topic:

Notes:

My Personal Thoughts:

_____

_____

_____

_____

_____

_____

_____

_____

Key Bible Verses:

_____

_____

_____

_____

_____

_____

_____

_____

_____

_____

*I urge you, first of all, to pray for all people. . .
and give thanks.*
1 TIMOTHY 2:1 NLT

Date and Time:

Place:

Today's Devotional Topic:

Notes:

My Personal Thoughts: ....

....

....

....

....

....

....

....

Key Bible Verses: ....

....

....

....

....

....

....

....

....

Teach me to do your will, for you are my God;
may your good Spirit lead me on level ground.
PSALM 143:10 NIV

Date and Time:

Place:

Today's Devotional Topic:

Notes:

My Personal Thoughts:

Key Bible Verses:

I will greatly rejoice in the LORD,
my soul shall be joyful in my God.
ISAIAH 61:10 KJV

Date and Time: _____

Place: _____

Today's Devotional Topic: _____

_____

Notes: _____

_____

_____

_____

_____

_____

_____

_____

_____

_____

My Personal Thoughts:

_____

_____

_____

_____

_____

_____

_____

Key Bible Verses:

_____

_____

_____

_____

_____

_____

_____

_____

_____

In every thing give thanks:
for this is the will of God in Christ Jesus concerning you.
1 THESSALONIANS 5:18 KJV

Date and Time:

Place:

Today's Devotional Topic:

Notes:

My Personal Thoughts:

Key Bible Verses:

Send forth your light and your truth, let them guide me;
let them bring me to your holy mountain,
to the place where you dwell.
Then will I go to the altar of God, to God,
my joy and my delight.
PSALM 43:3–4 NIV

Date and Time:

Place:

Today's Devotional Topic:

Notes:

My Personal Thoughts:

_____

_____

_____

_____

_____

_____

_____

Key Bible Verses:

_____

_____

_____

_____

_____

_____

_____

_____

_____

_____

O LORD, you are my God;
I will exalt you and praise your name,
for in perfect faithfulness you have done marvelous things,
things planned long ago.
ISAIAH 25:1 NIV

Date and Time:

Place:

Today's Devotional Topic:

Notes:

My Personal Thoughts:

Key Bible Verses:

I will give you a new heart and put a new spirit within you.
EZEKIEL 36:26 NKJV

Date and Time: ....

Place: ....

Today's Devotional Topic: ....

....

Notes: ....

....

....

....

....

....

....

....

....

....

My Personal Thoughts:

Key Bible Verses:

Take my yoke upon you and learn from me,
for I am gentle and humble in heart,
and you will find rest for your souls.
MATTHEW 11:29 NIV

Date and Time:

Place:

Today's Devotional Topic:

Notes:

My Personal Thoughts:

Key Bible Verses:

I will instruct you and teach you in the way you should go;
I will guide you with My eye.
PSALM 32:8 NKJV

Date and Time: _____

Place: _____

Today's Devotional Topic: _____

_____

Notes: _____

_____

_____

_____

_____

_____

_____

_____

_____

My Personal Thoughts:

_____

_____

_____

_____

_____

_____

_____

Key Bible Verses:

_____

_____

_____

_____

_____

_____

_____

_____

_____

Our soul waits for the LORD;
He is our help and our shield.
PSALM 33:20 NKJV

Date and Time:

Place:

Today's Devotional Topic:

Notes:

My Personal Thoughts:

_____

_____

_____

_____

_____

_____

_____

Key Bible Verses:

_____

_____

_____

_____

_____

_____

_____

_____

_____

The Lord is good to those who hope in him,
to those who seek him.
LAMENTATIONS 3:25 NCV

Date and Time: _____

Place: _____

Today's Devotional Topic: _____

_____

Notes: _____

_____

_____

_____

_____

_____

_____

_____

_____

_____

My Personal Thoughts:

_____

....

....

....

....

....

....

Key Bible Verses: ....

....

....

....

....

....

....

....

....

....

The LORD loves the just and will not forsake his faithful ones.
They will be protected forever.
PSALM 37:28 NIV

Date and Time:

Place:

Today's Devotional Topic:

Notes:

My Personal Thoughts:

_____

_____

_____

_____

_____

_____

_____

_____

_____

Key Bible Verses:

_____

_____

_____

_____

_____

_____

_____

_____

_____

_____

_____

Be still before the Lord, and wait patiently for him.
PSALM 37:7 NRSV

Date and Time: ....

Place: ....

Today's Devotional Topic: ....

....

Notes: ....

....

....

....

....

....

....

....

....

....

My Personal Thoughts:

_____

_____

_____

_____

_____

_____

_____

Key Bible Verses:

_____

_____

_____

_____

_____

_____

_____

_____

You have made known to me the path of life;
you will fill me with joy in your presence,
with eternal pleasures at your right hand.
PSALM 16:11 NIV

Date and Time:

Place:

Today's Devotional Topic:

Notes:

My Personal Thoughts:

Key Bible Verses:

From the fullness of his grace we have all received one blessing after another.
JOHN 1:16 NIV

Date and Time: ....
Place: ....
Today's Devotional Topic: ....
....

Notes: ....
....
....
....
....
....
....
....
....
....

My Personal Thoughts:

Key Bible Verses:

But thanks be to God, who always leads us in triumphal procession in Christ and through us spreads everywhere the fragrance of the knowledge of him. For we are to God the aroma of Christ among those who are being saved and those who are perishing.

2 CORINTHIANS 2:14–15 NIV

Date and Time:

Place:

Today's Devotional Topic:

Notes:

My Personal Thoughts:

Key Bible Verses:

But may all who seek you rejoice and be glad in you;
may those who love your salvation always say,
"The LORD be exalted!"
PSALM 40:16 NIV

Date and Time: ....

Place: ....

Today's Devotional Topic: ....

....

Notes: ....

....

....

....

....

....

....

....

....

....

My Personal Thoughts:

Key Bible Verses:

*The proof that we love God comes when we
keep his commandments
and they are not at all troublesome.*
1 JOHN 5:3 MSG

Date and Time: ....

Place: ....

Today's Devotional Topic: ....

....

Notes: ....

....

....

....

....

....

....

....

....

....

My Personal Thoughts:

Key Bible Verses:

If anyone obeys his word,
God's love is truly made complete in him.
This is how we know we are in him.
1 JOHN 2:5 NIV

Date and Time: ....

Place: ....

Today's Devotional Topic: ....

....

Notes: ....

....

....

....

....

....

....

....

....

....

....

My Personal Thoughts:

Key Bible Verses:

*You, LORD, give true peace to those who depend on you,
because they trust you.*
ISAIAH 26:3 NCV

Date and Time: ....

Place: ....

Today's Devotional Topic: ....

....

Notes: ....

....

....

....

....

....

....

....

....

....

My Personal Thoughts:

Key Bible Verses:

Our only goal is to please God.
2 CORINTHIANS 5:9 NCV

Date and Time: _____

Place: _____

Today's Devotional Topic: _____

_____

Notes: _____

_____

_____

_____

_____

_____

_____

_____

_____

_____

My Personal Thoughts:

_____

_____

_____

_____

_____

_____

_____

Key Bible Verses:

_____

_____

_____

_____

_____

_____

_____

_____

*Fear God and obey his commands,
for this is everyone's duty.*
ECCLESIASTES 12:13 NLT

Date and Time: ....

Place: ....

Today's Devotional Topic: ....

....

Notes: ....

....

....

....

....

....

....

....

....

....

My Personal Thoughts:

Key Bible Verses:

Seek his will in all you do,
and he will show you which path to take.
PROVERBS 3:6 NLT

Date and Time:

Place:

Today's Devotional Topic:

Notes:

My Personal Thoughts:

Key Bible Verses:

The eternal God is your refuge,
and underneath are the everlasting arms.
DEUTERONOMY 33:27 NIV

Date and Time:

Place:

Today's Devotional Topic:

Notes:

My Personal Thoughts:

_____

_____

_____

_____

_____

_____

_____

Key Bible Verses:

_____

_____

_____

_____

_____

_____

_____

_____

_____

God will generously provide all you need.
Then you will always have everything you need and
plenty left over to share with others.
2 CORINTHIANS 9:8 NLT

Date and Time:

Place:

Today's Devotional Topic:

Notes:

My Personal Thoughts:

Key Bible Verses:

[Jesus said,]
"Whoever serves me must follow me; and where I am,
my servant also will be.
My Father will honor the one who serves me."
JOHN 12:26 NIV

Date and Time:

Place:

Today's Devotional Topic:

Notes:

My Personal Thoughts:

_____

_____

_____

_____

_____

_____

_____

Key Bible Verses:

_____

_____

_____

_____

_____

_____

_____

_____

_____

_____

Trust the Lord with all your heart,
and don't depend on your own understanding.
PROVERBS 3:5 NCV

Date and Time:

Place:

Today's Devotional Topic:

Notes:

My Personal Thoughts:

Key Bible Verses:

Let the peace of Christ rule in your hearts,
since as members of one body you were called to peace.
COLOSSIANS 3:15 NIV

Date and Time:

Place:

Today's Devotional Topic:

Notes:

My Personal Thoughts: _____

_____

_____

_____

_____

_____

_____

_____

Key Bible Verses: _____

_____

_____

_____

_____

_____

_____

_____

_____

_____

_____

The LORD watches over all who love him.
PSALM 145:20 NIV

Date and Time: ....

Place: ....

Today's Devotional Topic: ....

....

Notes: ....

....

....

....

....

....

....

....

....

....

My Personal Thoughts:

Key Bible Verses:

God is our refuge and strength,
a very present help in trouble.
PSALM 46:1 NASB

Date and Time:

Place:

Today's Devotional Topic:

Notes:

My Personal Thoughts:

Key Bible Verses:

Let all that you do be done in love.
1 CORINTHIANS 16:14 NASB

Date and Time: ....

Place: ....

Today's Devotional Topic: ....

....

Notes: ....

....

....

....

....

....

....

....

....

....

....

My Personal Thoughts:

Key Bible Verses:

*Through Jesus, therefore, let us continually offer to God a
sacrifice of praise—the fruit of lips that confess his name.
And do not forget to do good and to share with others,
for with such sacrifices God is pleased.*
HEBREWS 13:15–16 NIV

Date and Time:

Place:

Today's Devotional Topic:

Notes:

My Personal Thoughts:

_____

_____

_____

_____

_____

_____

_____

_____

Key Bible Verses:

_____

_____

_____

_____

_____

_____

_____

_____

_____

Let the heavens rejoice, let the earth be glad; let them say among the nations, "The LORD reigns!" . . . Give thanks to the LORD, for he is good; his love endures forever.
1 CHRONICLES 16:31, 34 NIV

Date and Time: ....

Place: ....

Today's Devotional Topic: ....

....

Notes: ....

....

....

....

....

....

....

....

....

....

My Personal Thoughts:

Key Bible Verses:

Keep your eyes focused on what is right,
and look straight ahead to what is good.
PROVERBS 4:25 NCV

Date and Time: ....

Place: ....

Today's Devotional Topic: ....

....

Notes: ....

....

....

....

....

....

....

....

....

My Personal Thoughts:

_____

_____

_____

_____

_____

_____

_____

Key Bible Verses:

_____

_____

_____

_____

_____

_____

_____

_____

There shall be showers of blessing.
EZEKIEL 34:26 KJV

Date and Time:

Place:

Today's Devotional Topic:

Notes:

My Personal Thoughts:

....

....

....

....

....

....

....

Key Bible Verses:

....

....

....

....

....

....

....

....

....

The LORD is my strength and my shield;
my heart trusts in him, and I am helped.
My heart leaps for joy and I will give thanks to him in song.
PSALM 28:7 NIV

Date and Time: ....

Place: ....

Today's Devotional Topic: ....

....

Notes: ....

....

....

....

....

....

....

....

My Personal Thoughts:

_____

_____

_____

_____

_____

_____

_____

_____

Key Bible Verses:

_____

_____

_____

_____

_____

_____

_____

_____

_____

I will rejoice in the LORD,
I will joy in the God of my salvation.
HABAKKUK 3:18 KJV

Date and Time: ....

Place: ....

Today's Devotional Topic: ....

....

Notes: ....

....

....

....

....

....

....

....

....

....

My Personal Thoughts:

_____

_____

_____

_____

_____

_____

_____

Key Bible Verses:

_____

_____

_____

_____

_____

_____

_____

_____

_____

Be kind to each other, tenderhearted,
forgiving one another,
just as God through Christ has forgiven you.
EPHESIANS 4:32 NLT

Date and Time: ....

Place: ....

Today's Devotional Topic: ....

....

Notes: ....

....

....

....

....

....

....

....

....

My Personal Thoughts:

_____
_____
_____
_____
_____
_____
_____
_____

Key Bible Verses:

_____
_____
_____
_____
_____
_____
_____
_____
_____
_____

For God so loved the world,
that he gave his only begotten Son,
that whosoever believeth in him should not perish,
but have everlasting life.
JOHN 3:16 KJV

Date and Time:

Place:

Today's Devotional Topic:

Notes:

My Personal Thoughts:

Key Bible Verses:

Christ gives me the strength to face anything.
PHILIPPIANS 4:13 CEV

Date and Time:

Place:

Today's Devotional Topic:

Notes:

My Personal Thoughts:

Key Bible Verses:

Pray for each other so that you can live together whole and healed. The prayer of a person living right with God is something powerful to be reckoned with.
JAMES 5:16 MSG

Date and Time:

Place:

Today's Devotional Topic:

Notes:

My Personal Thoughts:

Key Bible Verses:

Once made perfect, [Christ] became the source of eternal salvation for all who obey him.
HEBREWS 5:9 NIV

Date and Time:

Place:

Today's Devotional Topic:

Notes:

My Personal Thoughts:

Key Bible Verses:

Trust in the Lord, and do good;
so you will live in the land, and enjoy security.
PSALM 37:3 NRSV

Date and Time:

Place:

Today's Devotional Topic:

Notes:

My Personal Thoughts:

_____

_____

_____

_____

_____

_____

_____

Key Bible Verses:

_____

_____

_____

_____

_____

_____

_____

_____

_____

_____

The LORD is my strength and my song; he has become my
salvation. He is my God, and I will praise him.
EXODUS 15:2 NIV

Date and Time:

Place:

Today's Devotional Topic:

Notes:

My Personal Thoughts:

Key Bible Verses:

Thanks be to God, which giveth us the victory through our Lord Jesus Christ.
1 CORINTHIANS 15:57 KJV

Date and Time: ....

Place: ....

Today's Devotional Topic: ....

....

Notes: ....

....

....

....

....

....

....

....

....

....

My Personal Thoughts:

Key Bible Verses: